Fiji
Travel Guide

Sightseeing, Hotel, Restaurant & Shopping Highlights

Thomas Austin

Table of Contents

Fiji

Formed out of volcanic mountains and tropical seas, Fiji's majestic coral reefs and friendly people attract tourists from around the world. Situated "on the way" from Hawaii to New Zealand, the archipelago includes 332 islands with about 110 of them inhabited. The 180° longitudinal line passes through Fiji twice – through the Vanua Levu and the Taveuni islands – placing Fiji in a time zone that is 'ahead' of most of the world.

Fiji has a diverse population with many Indian immigrants who represent almost half of Fiji. The other half is made up of Europeans and other Asians. The tourism industry forms the backbone of Fiji's economy and Fiji is one of the world's most beautiful travel destinations. You can choose from a budget hotel or a world-class luxury resort on an isolated island that attracts the rich and famous.

Fijian weddings and honeymoons are very popular and are even mentioned in the Guinness Book of World Records when five couples exchanged vows at 41,000 feet on the way to Fiji on a Fiji Airways flight! Family resorts featuring kids' activities are widespread throughout Fiji making it a very popular destination for families and other categories of tourists.

Culture

Like several other Pacific islands, Fiji has a strong Christian community and many Indians are Hindu or Muslim. English is the official language, although Fijian and Hindustani languages are also spoken extensively. Businesses and shops are closed on Sundays, with church services starting around 6 PM the day before. Some businesses celebrate a Saturday Sabbath, so check the hours of operation beforehand.

Though Fiji is a tropical nation, beachwear is generally restricted to the beach. In the towns and city's do dress modestly. A good rule of thumb is to take a cue from the locals as to what is considered an appropriate outfit for any occasion. It is recommended that you cover your shoulders when visiting towns or villages. It is also considered respectful that one's knees be covered, especially when visiting a church. This is true for both men and women. If you intend to visit a church and do not have an appropriate piece of clothing handy, check with the locals who will often lend sarongs for such visits.

Wearing a hat may be misinterpreted as an insult to the chief of the village. You should also not touch your head. When visiting a house in the village, you may be asked to remove your shoes. To blend in with the locals, gift an inexpensive item to the chief of the village. Be aware that villagers often shake heads and ask personal questions like 'are you married?' or 'how many children do you have?' etc.

Location & Orientation

Also known as the Fiji Islands, Fiji is a Melanesian country located in the South Pacific Ocean. There are several modes of transport to get in and out of Fiji as well as to explore the Fiji mainland.

Located to the west of Fiji's main island Viti Levu, Nadi International Airport is Fiji's primary international airport. Some international flights also operate out of the Suva Island. The most popular airlines chosen to get into Fiji is the Fiji Airways, a large majority of which is owned by Fiji. Fiji Airways operate from Los Angeles, Honolulu, Hong Kong and several other cities around the world. Apart from Fiji Airways, Korean Air also operates flights between Nadi International Airport and Seoul. Travelers from New Zealand can fly on Air New Zealand operated flights from Christchurch and Auckland. Seasonal flights also operate out of Wellington. Several flights operate from Australia.

An alternate mode of transport is across the deep blue Pacific waters. Fiji's shores can be accessed by a few boats from Australia.

Within Fiji, there are a number of public transport options that include buses, private taxis and share taxis. Bus tickets are cheap, costing only about $1-2 from the Colo-i-Suva station to the Suva main bus stand. Share taxis, white mini vans which wait until they pick up about 6-8 passengers, also charge reasonably. The average cost of a share taxi from the Nadi bus stand to Suva is about $17-$18. Hiring a private taxi from Sigatoka to Suva Airport costs about $80-85. While on the Viti Levu or the Taveuni mainland, as far as possible, hire taxis with meters. Ensure that the driver turns on the meter as rates on metered taxis are a lot cheaper as compared to negotiated rates. Taxis charge about $8-10 to ferry you from resorts along Nadi beach to downtown. A trip from the resorts along Nadi beach to the Nadi International Airport costs about $12-14.

Climate & When to Visit

Fiji Islands experience a sunny, tropical climate and are known to have two seasons. From May to November there is a "less hot" climate, with temperatures in the range of 19° to 29° Celsius (66° to 85°Fahrenheit). Temperatures from the months of December to April are much hotter ranging from 22° to 33° Celsius (71° to 91° Fahrenheit).

Fiji experiences heavy rains during its hotter months of December to April. The relatively colder months of May through November are the best months to visit Fiji. Rainfall and humidity are lower during these months. Temperatures are milder and there is less risk of natural hazards like cyclones. However, because of these reasons, tourist influx to Fiji is at its peak during these months and hence airfare and accommodations are pricier. It is recommended that you book in advance to save on travel costs.

Sightseeing Highlights

Viti Levu

Fiji's largest island, Viti Levu is home to the adventure capital of Fiji – Suva. The Natadola beach, a beautiful palm fringed white sand beach on this island, is touted as one of the best beaches in the world. The Natadola, a picture perfect falcate of white powdery sand, leads to some spectacular cliffs and exotic scenery. Striking clear skies and blue lagoons entice plenty of local swimmers and international tourists.

Horses are also available for hire on the beach – both gentle rides for young kids as well as seasoned horses for adult horse rides. Be prepared to indulge in heavy bargaining with the horse ride vendors as the first prices stated are usually opportunistic. Treks along the island cater to all levels of fitness.

Local Fijians often offer massage services along the beach for a nominal fee. If you are lucky, you might find a massage tent set up along the beach. Stunning views of the sunset coupled with aromatic massages are definitely a do-not-miss on the traveler's itinerary.

Another popular attraction at Viti Levu is the Natadola Bay Championship Golf Course that offers incredible views and a challenging design. Most resorts on the island offer shuttles every half hour that can drive you up the hills to the golf course. If you are not into golf, you can still go for a spin in the golf cart around the golf course simply for the spectacular views that the course offers. The onsite café offers delicious meals at an affordable rate. It is recommended that you book course tours in advance as tickets and tours are limited. The Natadola Bay Championship Golf Course can be contacted at (679) 673 3500.

The Fiji Rivers, located along Upper Navua and Luva River in Pacific Harbour within Viti Levu, offer sea kayaking excursions and whitewater rafting opportunities for adventure enthusiasts of all ages and fitness levels. Several adventure activity operators offer day-long highland river adventure trips along the Luva River.

Paradise Beach is said to offer the best value of money through its day-long trips that include mouthwatering BBQ lunches, great snorkeling sites, rain forest walks, waterfalls and hammocks set up at the beach. Tours are usually limited to small groups and cater to families and couples alike. Tour operators set up large shelters that include all basic facilities, relaxing live music, BBQ lunches, hammocks and more.

The Kula Eco Park, located opposite to the Outrigger on the Lagoon resort, is a multiple award-winning establishment on the island. Having won the Phoenix Award in 2012, the Kula Eco Park is Fiji's only wildlife park that hosts native reptiles, birds, turtles, live corals, tropical fish, bats and more. Turtle feeding sessions are held at 11 AM, 1 PM and 3: 30 PM every day and if you are in the vicinity, you can even engage in a turtle feeding session arranged by the local coordinators. The park is open every day from 10 AM to 4 PM and advance booking is recommended. The Kula Eco Park can be contacted at (679) 6500 505. Tickets can also be booked online at http://www.fijiwild.com/.

One very popular activity while in Viti Levu is the Zip line adventure which is held at Wainadoi, Pacific Harbour. If you are looking for something different to do in your trip, then the Zip Line is highly recommended. Catering to all ages, skilled guides at the site are extremely friendly and help ease any fears you might have. The average cost of a package, inclusive of pick up and drop, is about $90 per head. You can book your tickets online at http://zip-fiji.com/ or call (679) 930 0545.

While in Viti Levu, you should try to visit the Paradise Fiji waterfalls in Sigatoka. Here, you can visit the homes of the village chiefs, partake in some traditional Fijian ceremonies and hear fascinating tales about local fables, superstitions and ancient practices of witch craft and folklore. The Kava drink offered as part of the ceremony can be slightly intoxicating, so it is recommended that you consume it in limited quantities. You can enjoy refreshing dips in the waterfall pools and lagoons, relax and enjoy the cathartic waters and soak in the serenity of nature. The path to get to the waterfalls involves a 40 minute walk wading through shallow streams. Hence, strong waterproof footwear is highly recommended. Croc sandals are also available for hire for about $5 a pair. Tour companies that organize visits usually include picnic lunches as part of the trip, however it is recommended that you confirm with the tour company before you embark on the trip.

One of the most exhilarating sights while on the island is the Beqa Firewalkers. Witnessed both on Beqa Island as well as along the Pacific Harbour, Beqa firewalkers are men who walk slowly over burning hot-white stones and coals and profess to experience no burns or pains whatsoever.

Nadi

The third largest metropolis in Fiji, Nadi is located to the west of the main island of Viti Levu. It is one of the largest towns in the Fiji Islands and usually the first tourist stop on Fiji. This teeming metropolis is an international hub for travelers and boasts of a large number of eateries, pubs and shopping districts. Located in close proximity to Mamanucas and the Denarau Island, Nadi is an ideal place to set up base while in Fiji.

One of Nadi's most spectacular beaches is the Nadi beach, a wide strand of white sand perfect for lazing around in the sun and watching sunsets on the beach. The neighboring Natadola beach is another stunning beach popular for body surfing activities and swimming. A large number of tours and adventure activities take off from these beaches or from the town of Nadi that allow tourists easy access to the nearby islands of Yasawas and Mamanucas. While here, do try your hand at activities like scuba diving, snorkeling, or hiking. Kids can also participate in kayaking and windsurfing along the beach waters. The Coral Coast Scenic Railway offers great insight into the Fijian landscape and is a great way to experience the coastal network.

Nadi also hosts the largest Hindu temple in the southern hemisphere – the Sri Siva Subramaniya where the temple front provides an exciting foreground against a dramatic hilly backdrop. The temple hosts several woodcarvings from India along with the artists who designed the temple, its vibrant colourful façade, and spectacular ceiling frescos. The Waqadra Botanical Gardens are also located on the Nadi Island.

Vuda Lookout, Sabeto Valley & Sleeping Giant

A half day tour, travelling from the Vuda Lookout to the Sabeto Valley and the Sleeping Giant Orchid collection is a beautiful way to spend your time while in Nadi.

Tour operators provide you friendly and professional tour guides for the duration of your trip. Well versed with the history and geography of the islands, these tour guides speak fluent English, and are always available to answer any questions you might have about the places you will be visiting as part of the tour. The Vuda Lookout is a famed spot on the island that offers 360° views of the island, the mountains ranges on the west, Nadi International Airport and the Yasawas. The lookout also provides plenty of opportunities for some spectacular photography. From the Vuda Lookout, you would be able to see as far as the Nadi Bay and the Yasawas islands.

From Nadi's scenic heartland, you then step into the beautiful valley of Sabeto and into the Sleeping Giant Orchid Garden – Fiji's largest and most diverse orchid collection. Open from Monday-Saturday, the entry free to these gardens is about $10 per head. The tour then takes you through to Viseisei Village, the landing site of the first Fijians on the island. Here, you can explore the village on foot and browse through some beautiful handmade handicraft displays. While here, you can relax in a Fijian Bure – a traditional hut made with wood, straw, hay, and grass. At the Bure, enjoy a chilled glass of tropical fruit juice and some seasonal fruits from the local orchards.

The half day tour also includes a visit to the local Namaka markets where you can purchase indigenous items, authentic handicrafts and traditional trinkets, as well as to the Nadi temple on the island. The half day tour is usually priced at about $65 per adult and $35 per child. Infants are admitted free.

Denarau Islands

Boasting of eight different resorts to choose from, Denarau Island is a man-made paradise island located off the coast of Viti Levu. Only 2.55 square kilometers in area, and located 5 kilometers north-west to Nadi, the unique feature of the island is that many of the resorts are integrated and offer a variety of shared activities across resorts. You can choose from world class golf, scuba diving, parasailing and tennis. Excellent shopping districts are also located on the island in addition to some first-rate dining options that cater to all kinds of travelers – from families to honeymooner couples – and fit all budgets.

Port Denarau also hosts the Fiji International Jazz and Blues festival, making Fiji an international festival center. Multiple resorts on the island also host the South Pacific Food and Wine Festival; so if you are in the vicinity while the festival is in town, be sure to attend. During the festival, international chefs explore and experiment with the flavours and the food of the South Pacific. Restaurants on the island offer thrilling indoor and outdoor dining experiences, in addition to serving up international cuisines.

Denarau Island is only 8 minutes away from the Nadi International airport and a short ride away from the mainland. Taxi rides are very reasonable and most of the hotel resorts offer free shuttles to the mainland. While on Denarau, you can charter private boats and have a swim in the ocean, surf the waves, snorkel and explore the stunning coral reefs surrounded by breathtaking marine life, visit beautiful spots along the shore, island hop, enjoy game fishing or go for a Jet Ski coastal run.

Denarau Islands are also often the starting point for many a day tour and adventure activities along the coast. While in Denarau, you can embark on day long cruises that take you to Castaway Island, South Sea Islands, and even the Mamanucas Islands and include BBQ lunches, snorkeling time, and island exploration. The average cost of a day cruise is about $100 per person.

Mamanucas Islands

A volcanic archipelago of about 20 islands located to the west of Nadi town and to the south of Yasawas, the Mamanucas islands boast of crystal clear waters, sandy beaches lined with palm trees, and live spectacular coral reefs. The islands are also host to a number of villages and resorts and offer an idyllic environment to snorkel and swim. However, one must exercise caution and be aware that during hide tide, the waters of the Pacific Ocean cover about seven of these islands.

Island hopper helicopters or float planes offer the fastest way to reach the islands. However, helicopter hires are usually extremely expensive. Free buses can also be boarded from any of the major resorts near Nadi town or from the airport. These buses ferry passengers to the Port Denarau or the Denarau Marina which is 20 minutes away from the Nadi International Airport. One can visit the Mamanucas Islands as part of a day trip from the Denarau Marina.

Large catamarans ferry about 200 passengers to different islands within the Mamanucas. Travel times depend on which island you are travelling to. Catamarans depart from the marina, thrice a day, at 9 AM, 12:15 PM and 3:15 PM. Water taxis, or small aluminum boats, also service these islands and are good for groups of people travelling to the same destination. Day cruises from the Marina cost about $100 per person.

Those who remember the scenic beauty and landscapes from the movie Castaway would be thrilled to know that Monuriki, an island from this archipelago, was the location where the film was shot. Tom Hanks spent many a movie moment camping on these islands. The Mamanucas have also been featured in several TV shows including Treasure Island and The Resort.

Mamanucas islands offer accommodation to all range of travelers – starting from backpackers/budget conscious travelers to high end luxury travelers. While on these islands, you can engage in a host of activities including and not restricted to swimming, snorkeling, sailing, kayaking, coral viewing through semi-submersible water vehicles, diving with reef sharks, hiking, visiting villages, sunset cruising, jet skiing, island hopping, paddle boarding, dolphin watching, cultural village trips, banana boating, game fishing, mini-golf and windsurfing. Interested travelers and groups of tourists also often embark on missions to discover secluded beaches. Several resorts also offer exotic spa treatments. If you would like to experience an idyllic setting and are in the mood for calm and quiet, the Tokoriki and Navini islands provide opportunities for serene walks, good indigenous bird watching and decent fishing spots.

Located on the sunnier and drier side of the archipelago, the Mamanucas experience warmer temperatures, less tropical climates and much less rain. Enjoying popularity for its sun and sand, its palm fringed beaches, lagoons and water sports, Mamanucas is a much loved destination among international travelers.

All-Day Whales Tale Cruises

The all-day Whales Tale Cruise is a one day cruise trip that covers five different islands in the Fijian archipelago giving you a taste of these islands. Sailing through the blue lagoons, the cruise sails along the Mamanucas beaches and takes you to your own uninhabited island paradise.

The cruise includes pick up and drop off from centrally located places like Port Denarau, Nadi, Lautoka and the Coral Coast and includes activities like snorkeling, underwater explorations and more.

Most Whale Tale Cruises serve champagne along with continental breakfast during departure. Gourmet lunch buffets are also served on your own private exclusive island where you disembark during the day. If you have a special occasion you would like to celebrate on the cruise, say a honeymoon, birthday or an anniversary, chefs on the cruise ship indulge you and bake special occasion cakes for you and your group of travelers. The cruise also includes unlimited drinks from a selection of soft drinks, fruit juices, beer and wine.

While on the cruise, you also get an opportunity to take the wheel and guide the cruise along its charted path. There's onboard entertainment on the cruise in addition to entertainment that is arranged on the private island where you disembark, which makes the entire trip a fun-filled one. Cruise ships stack enough snorkeling gear for all guests onboard; guides on the cruise would let you know the best snorkeling sites where you can explore the colourful reef and corals underwater. Some tour operators also include activities like scuba diving, beach volleyball, glass bottomed boat tours, kayaking and more. Additional activities like massages and motorized activities while on the island, are charged extra. Cruise ships and tour operators ensure that the number of guests onboard a cruise ship are limited so as to give you the maximum benefit and feel of a personalized island experience.

The average cost of a Whales Tale Day cruise is about $110 per adult and about $70 for juniors aged between 12 and 16 years old. Tickets for children aged between 5 and 11 years cost about $55 per head and infants, aged 4 years or younger, are admitted free of charge.

Navua River Village & Kava Ceremony

The Kava Ceremony at the Navua River Village offers you an excellent opportunity to witness and experience the indigenous Fijian culture, interact with village locals and learn about their customs and traditions. Including hotel pick up and drop off, the day starts off with a leisurely boat ride up the picturesque Navua River. Winding through traditional villages, the motor boat makes its way through untouched beautiful waterfalls and gorges which are a visual treat to watch. Along the river, you are presented with countless opportunities to click photographs of the spectacular scenery that you pass by.

Once at the Navua River Village, you can partake in a traditional Kava ceremony which includes consumption of the lightly intoxicating drink called Kava. In Fijian culture, kava also known as grog or yaqona, is regarded as the drink of life and is drunk morning, noon and night, within the confines of one's home or in the village hall. Consuming the drink is regarded as a form of welcome and no traditional ceremony is complete without the drink. As part of the ceremony, local stories are told, folklore is read and jokes are exchanged. The Kava ceremony often functions as peace talks among warring factions in the village.

After the Kava ceremony, you get to enjoy a traditional Fijian lunch prepared by the local villagers followed by idyllic relaxation along the waterfalls and swimming pools near the falls. You also have plenty of opportunity and time to click pictures of the scenic beauty surrounding the village and of the indigenous village ambience. Guides allocated to each group speak fluent English and will be available to answer any questions you might have. Tours culminate at the same point as your departure point the morning of the trip.

Typical hours of operation for day tours are 7:30-8:00 AM hotel pickups (depending on which hotel you stay in) to 6:30 PM drop off. The average cost of a Navua River Village tour including the Kava Ceremony costs about $90-100 per adult depending on the tour operator you pick.

Fiji Sunset Dinner Cruise & Cultural Show

The Fiji Sunset Dinner Cruise has been touted as the most popular night time cruise across all of Fiji. Setting off from the Denarau Marina, Fiji Sunset Dinner Cruises usually start at about 5:00 PM - 5:30 PM depending on the season. During winters, cruises depart early at about 5 PM while in summers with long days, cruises depart around 5:30 PM. Hotel pickups commence before the cruise departure, so it is recommended that you check with your tour operator as to the exact time of pick up from your hotel.

Sunset Dinner Cruises start off with a welcome drink, a complimentary cocktail in most cases, followed by a scrumptious BBQ dinner of steak or fish. For an additional charge, you also have the option to upgrade your dinner to freshly caught lobster. The lobster upgrade entails chargrilled lobster served in half shells along with seasonal exotic vegetables served on the side. Dinner also includes salads and dessert options; vegetarian options are also available on prior request. Dinner is followed by complimentary tea or coffee; alcoholic beverages can be purchased from the bar.

Wining and dining with the Pacific Ocean as a backdrop, you can listen to islander ballads sung and performed by crews onboard. Most cruises also include an authentic Fiji cultural show giving you an insight into the Fijian culture and traditions.

The three hour long sunset cruise gives you plenty of time to soak in picture perfect views of the ocean, admire the mesmerizing sunset scenery as the horizon turns from blue to pinks and orange, enjoy the onset of twilight and watch the sun go down in all its splendour. Through its course, the cruise winds through idyllic tropical islands and deep blue lagoons nestled amid the glittering waters of the Pacific Ocean.

As this is a much talked about cruise, it is recommended that you book tickets in advance. With a large number of tour operators organizing dinner cruises, you will have many options to choose from and prices will be competitive. The average cost of a Sunset Dinner cruise is about $75 per adult and about $50 per child. Infants younger than 2 years old are admitted free. Private charter vessels are also available if required, though private charters can be pretty expensive.

Sawailau Limestone Caves Trip

The Sawailau limestone caves are caves that are located on the Sawa-i-Lau Island within the Fijian archipelago. The Sawa-i-Lau Island, also known as Sawailau Island, is a small island situated off the southern tip of the Yasawas. The 1980 famed movie, the Blue Lagoon, starring Brooke Shields, was shot here.

The Sawailau Limestone caves is a set of three different caves. The first and the main limestone cave has a huge chamber with a 15 meter deep swimming pool within the cave. The highlight of any visit to the cave is to be able to swim within the cave, between the limestone walls on each side. Along the limestone walls, you will find ancient inscriptions which have also been examined by archeologists.

The main cave is easily accessible through low tide, but one needs to swim under a rocky curtain and through an underwater tunnel to get to the other cave. The water in the tunnel is clear and only a couple degrees cooler than the water in the Pacific Ocean. There are two chambers within the cave – the first one is the tall atrium of the outer chamber which lets in light from a huge opening in the cave's ceiling and the second chamber is the smaller inner sanctum which is pitch dark and lets no light in.

The second cave is called the Qara Ni Bukete, also known as the pregnancy cave. Legend has it that the cave doesn't allow any pregnant woman in, who is trying to hide her pregnancy. The third cave is called the Qara Ni Kasivi or the Spitting Cave. There is also a local shell market outside the caves which offers tourists an opportunity to purchase little keepsakes of their trip to the caves. Once out of the caves, several tour guides offer you the option to go snorkeling or diving. You can also jump on to a jet ski and tour the waters surrounding the island.

Tour guides are usually excellent at their job and very friendly, holding your head under the water and guiding you expertly so you do not accidently hit your head on the rocks while you try to swim underwater. Armed with torches, the guides lead you to the far end of the second cave where you sit on ledges and take in stories and legends about the caves. If you want to take photographs, make sure you take along waterproof cameras. The average cost of a trip to the Limestone caves is about $28-30 per adult.

Coral Coast

Fiji's Coral Coast is one of the most sought after destinations in the Fijian archipelago. With a large number of luxury resorts located right along the beachfront, Coral Coast is frequented by a large number of tourists wanting to stay right on the beach. While here, there are a host of activities you can indulge in.

At the Outrigger on the Lagoon, you can work with creative staff and create your own Fijian jewelry, artifacts and island wear. You can also embark on a diving tour from any of the resorts along the coast and experience a whole day of diving and snorkeling. Several tour operators also operate glass-bottomed boats where you can view beautiful colourful fish and corals from the confines of the boat without having to get your feet wet.

An alternate much-enjoyed activity is the Sigatoka River Safari, an authentic Fiji safari that teaches you all about Fiji's history and provides you with an unparalleled cultural experience. While here, you can also pay a visit to the Tauvani Hill Fort, an ancient fort in Fiji which is now also an archeological site.

Recommendations for the Budget Traveller

Places to Stay

Waidroka Bay Resort, Korovisilou

Deuba, Korovisilou, Viti Levu, 323
Tel: (679) 330 4605
http://www.waidroka.com/

With four different rooms available, Waidroka Bay Resort offers excellent accommodation.

With adventure packages at extremely reasonable rates. Located 2 hours from the airport and only 20 minutes away from Pacific Harbour's adventure capital, Waidroka Bay Resort offers rooms ranging from approximately $130-$140 a night for accommodation homes away from the beach to deluxe ocean front bungalows priced at about $160-$180 per night.

Raffles Gateway Hotel

Nadi Airport,
Fiji Islands
Tel: (679) 672 2444
http://www.rafflesgateway.com/

Conveniently located just 8 kilometers from Nadi downtown and within walking distance to the Nadi International Airport, the Raffles Gateway Hotel features a state of the art kitchen, stunning gardens and sweeping landscapes. The hotel is also the winner of the Best 3 Star Budget Hotel category in the AON Excellence Tourism awards of 2007. Rooms are priced at about $80-$95 per night.

The Terraces Apartments, Denarau

Port Denarau,
Denarau Islands,
Viti Levu
Tel: (679) 675 0557
http://www.theterraces.com.fj/

Located in the heart of the Denarau Island, the Terraces is located only a short walk to the Marina, great restaurants and value shopping. Featuring a 25 meter swimming pool and access to the Denarau Golf Course, the Terraces single bedroom, double bedroom and three bedroom apartments are only 20 minutes away from Denarau downtown and 10 minutes away from Nadi downtown. Apartment prices range from about $125 - $150 per night.

Bedarra Beach Inn

Sunset Strip, Korotoga, Sigatoka, Viti Levu
Tel: (679) 650 0476
http://www.bedarrafiji.com/

Offering a peaceful lagoon beach, exotic fresh water pools, car hire and Wi-Fi Internet access, Bedarra Beach Inns offer personalized friendly customer service with spacious accommodation, appealing cuisine and special attention at affordable prices. Room prices range from about $80-$90 per night.

Natadola Beach Resort

Maro Road,
Viti Levu
Tel: (679) 672 1001
http://www.natadola.com/

Offering all tide swimming and snorkeling activities at both ends of the beach, a spectacular fresh water swimming pool, a beautiful restaurant and fantastic accommodation, Natadola offers complete privacy with only 11 suites at the resort. Located only an hour's drive away from the Nadi International Airport, Natadola's suites are priced at about $110-$120 per night.

Places to Eat & Drink

Bulaccino Cafe & Hemisphere Bar

Nataly Building, Namaka, Nadi, Viti Levu
Tel: (679) 672 8638
http://bulaccino.com/

Open for breakfast and lunch all seven days of the week from 6 AM onwards, and for Dinner Tuesdays-Sundays, Bulaccino's is the restaurant of choice among many Fijian tourists for its mouthwatering breads, cakes and pastries.

Prices of appetizers range from $6-$10 and main course dishes start at about $15.

Ocean Terrace Restaurant

77 Sunset Strip, Bedarra Beach Inn, Korotogo,
Sigatoka, Viti Levu
Tel: (679) 650 0476
http://www.bedarrafiji.com/cuisine

Located on the Coral Coast, Ocean Terrace offers
international cuisines, boasts of an impressive staff and
provides the perfect holiday ambience. Providing easy
access to reefs, snorkeling activities and paddling, Ocean
Terrace Restaurant offers great value for money. The
coconut based dishes and Kokada – the local fish - entrees
come highly recommended. Appetizers are priced at
about $8-$15 while main dishes range from $20-$30.

IVI Restaurant at Outrigger on the Lagoon

Outrigger on the Lagoon, Sigatoka, Viti Levu
Tel: (679) 650 0044
http://www.outrigger.com/hotels-resorts/fiji/viti-levu/outrigger-on-the-lagoon-fiji

Situated adjacent to a hundred year old Ivy tree, the IVI
restaurant offers Pacific Continental cuisine, served Fijian
style.

Do bear in mind that the restaurant is not recommended for children 12 years and younger. Dinner is served from 6 PM – 10:30 PM and dressing is smart casual. The IVI Restaurant won the AON Excellence in Tourism award in the 'Best Fine Dining' category.

Sundowner Bar & Grill

Outrigger on the Lagoon,
Sigatoka, Viti Levu
Tel: (679) 650 0044
http://www.castawayfiji.com/dining/sundowner-pizza-bar

Open for breakfast from 9 AM onwards, the Sundowner bar offers gourmet wood-fired pizzas with thin, crisp bases and scrumptious topping alternatives. Breakfast pizzas, gourmet pizzas and all day drinks are also available as part of the dinner menus at night. Happy hour is between 5 PM and 7 PM. Evenings are designated as childfree environments. Free Kids Clubs and baby-sitting services are available for families for children.

Mamacita Mexican Restaurant & Bar

Worldmark by Wyndham Resort
Denarau Island

Located in the Wyndham resort and introducing a style of cuisine not previously available on the island, Mamacita offers authentic Mexican dishes and boasts of the largest tequila collection in all of Fiji.

Offering both indoor seating and an outdoor deck area seating, Mamacita's grand feature is the open bar area surrounded by water on all sides. A family friendly restaurant, Mamacita's offers classic Mexican favourites like nachos, burritos, fajitas and guacamole.

Places to Shop

Suvo Curio & Handicraft Center

Stinson Parade City Centre, Suvo
Tel: (679) 331 3433

With endless stalls and fantastic deals, the Suvo Curio and Handicraft Center is an interesting place to amble through. Stall vendors do engage in some heavy bargaining so be ready to bargain if you wish to purchase items. Stall vendors also like to convince tourists about the authenticity of the artifacts, however, not all of them are genuine.

D Solanki

Town Center, Suva
Tel: (679) 885 0025

D Solanki's stores offer beautifully done, double stitched saris and tailor made suits as well as traditional Fijian costumes. You will also find reasonably priced western wear at Solanki's.

Hot Bread Kitchen

Town Center,
Savusavu,
Suva
Tel: (679) 331 3919

Host to quite a few bakery shops, grocery stores, and a well-stocked supermarket, Savusavu is a good place to shop for fruits, vegetables, and bread. Baking fresh loaves of bread on a daily basis, the Hot Bread Kitchen is a popular destination for food shoppers and enthusiasts.

Free Shop

Town Center, Suva
Tel: (679) 359 3201

Exhibiting jewelry, clothing and crafts made by local artisans and craftsmen, the Free Shop is an establishment supported by the United Nations Development Program. Every item displayed in the Free Shop is supported by a write-up that provides background information about the item.

ROC Market

Loftus Street, Victoria Parade Center,
Suva

Items sold at the ROC Market in Suva include clothes, accessories, food and potted plants, books and paintings that are sold at good prices. Offering a variety of second hand books, the ROC market has seen a steady increase in footfall. Stalls change on a weekly basis so return visits can be made.

CPSIA information can be obtained
at www.ICGtesting.com
Printed in the USA
LVOW04s1220210216
476057LV00036B/1068/P